GROWING IN THE DARK

NACQUEL ROBERTS CLAUDE

ISBN: 978-1-7357952-1-8

Printed by Power Of Purpose Publishing
www.PopPublishing.com
Atlanta, Ga. 30326

CONTENTS

PRECIOUS TREASURES GROW IN DARK PLACES

It is at the darkest moments in our lives that we will see the breaking of dawn!

The desire to write this book has lingered with me for over five years. However, I was not inspired to write until this season.

One of the things that I have discovered over the last five years of my journey in life is that I was going through a process, and that God would eventually use my story and its outcome all for His glory.

Today, I am an overcomer, and my life serves as a testimony that God is faithful; His ways are past finding out, and He will never abandon His own.

No doubt, there are many challenges that we will face in life, however, we can overcome them all and be victorious.

One of the purposes of this book is that you would understand that God is with you in the darkest seasons of your life: that dark seasons of your life will lead you to your wealthy place, if you do not give up.

Maybe your life is in a dark place - maybe your marriage is on the brink of failing, or your health is failing you. I believe with every fiber of my being that God has a great purpose for you, but you will only reap the blessings or the benefits of His goodness if you put your faith in Him.

Galatians 6:9 "Let us not become weary in doing good, for at the proper time, we will reap a harvest if we do not give up."

It's the darkest moments of your life that will purify, sanctify, and stretch you until you feel like you will break, but this is all part of the process!

Remember, Jesus was led into the wilderness to be tempted by the devil.

Such a process comes only to those who are handpicked by God for a special task.

Therefore, when the Holy Spirit leads us into such dark places or a wilderness experiences, it is because He has an eternal purpose in mind just for us. He wants to bless us and give us a life that will give us great joy, peace, and satisfaction and in which purpose will be fulfilled.

Matthew 4:1 "Then Jesus was led by the Spirit into the wilderness to be tempted by the devil."

As you read through each page of this book, I want you to think of this as a tool or a weapon to encourage you to stay in the process and to overcome every challenge you might face in life.

Just know that you are an overcomer; yes, you are!

Know that God is for you!

I believe as you continue reading this book, the Holy spirit will speak to you, and your life will never be the same - you will be transformed, and your mind will be renewed.

You will understand that you are in a process, and that God can use your situations for His divine purpose, if you allow Him. Further, remember that ".... all things (you face in your life will) work together for your good because you are called of God and He has a divine purpose for you. Would you accept it?

The challenges we face in life humble us and teach us lifelong lessons that can never be learned from an institution or your greatest mentor.

If you refuse to give up in the process, you will gain fuel for greater success.

I am reminded of the great President Theodore Roosevelt who lost both his mother and wife on the same day. Imagine the terrible dark period of grief he must have endured; however, he became a war hero and a very powerful president of the United States, despite his challenges.

I believe, with all my heart that you, like President Theodore Roosevelt, was born and is destined for a great mission in life. Accept it. Come into agreement with God!

CHAPTER 1

THE CHINESE BAMBOO TREE

If you have never heard about the Chinese bamboo tree before, let me be the first to share with you what I have learned.

The process of the Chinese bamboo starts from a very small seed. Knowing the benefits of this tree that it would one day become great; the farmer carefully plants the seed in the best soil and waters that spot daily. He does everything he needs to do in order to see to the seed's manifestation to greatness; he watches attentively year after year – but for an entire first year, nothing happens.

No doubt, this is how we tend to feel in life: *I have been giving my all. I live a fasted life; I spend hours in prayer; I study God's Word day and night; I have even sowed that significant seed and named it as the preacher said I should. I'm doing everything right, but nothing is springing forth; there is no manifestation.*

As a result of not seeing the product, day by day we become bombarded with thoughts that tend to weigh us down; such thoughts as :-

There is no way I will ever make it

- *There is no way I will ever get married.*
- *There is no way I can stay married.*
- *There is no way my children will serve God wholeheartedly.*
- *There is no way I will ever get out of debt.*
- *There is no way I will ever complete college....*

However, God wants us to renew our minds and not to focus on what we DO NOT SEE. The word of God tells us in Romans 8:20 "but if we hope for that we see not, then do we with patience wait for it." Paul also teaches that the "spiritual mind" is life and peace. Not until our minds are renewed by the Word of God, will we develop the spirit of endurance to wait until we see the manifestation.

Find out what the bible has to say about your situation and confess the word of God over your life in that area daily. Once your mind has been renewed, you will discover your entire life changing for better right before your eyes.

As the story continue .... The second year comes, and as the farmer continues to wait for the Chinese bamboo tree to grow, yet again, nothing happens.

He decides that he will continue to water and fertilize it.

We must be patient in the process and remain consistent. When you struggle to give up, wait for the Lord. Your strength will be renewed as you wait.

Whenever we decide to embrace life's processes, we will realize that patience and grace is often required.

It is the dark moments of our lives that God uses to develop us, to show us how we can rely fully on Him.

God wants us to 'lean not' on our own human understanding, but to look to Him for direction and guidance. However, if we choose to be impatient and drop out of the race, then we will lose out on all that God is trying to teach us about discipline, faith, courage, and perseverance.

Let me admonish you not to become overwhelmed with the big picture, maybe it will even take years to get you to that point, but focus rather on God and all that He wants to do in and through your life.

I wholeheartedly believe that there's a reason that God sometimes allows the delays. God often gives us bite-sized portions because He knows just how much we can handle at one time.

Isaiah 40:31 – "But they who wait for the LORD shall renew their strength, they shall mount up with wings like eagles, they shall run and not be weary, they shall walk and not faint."

James 5:7-11 – *"Be patient, therefore, brethren, until the coming of the Lord. Behold, the farmer waits for the precious fruit of the earth, being patient over it until it receives the early and the late rain. You also be patient. Establish your hearts, for the coming of the Lord is at hand. Do not grumble, brethren, against one another, that you may not be judged; behold, the Judge is standing at the doors. As an example of suffering and patience, brethren, take the prophets who spoke in the name of the Lord. Behold, we call those happy who were steadfast."*

In the third year, the farmer continues to water the seed he planted.

He gives it the best fertilizer on the market; he even goes as far as getting advice from his neighbors. Perhaps this is just one of the biggest mistakes that he can make.

Sometimes, in order to win it must be done in secret.

You cannot tell everyone your dream or your next move in life. Just like the farmer, we get excited and anxious at the same time. We look to our family and friends for advice or support, and just one negative word spoken can throw us off course.

Let me be the bearer of bad news for a second, not everyone likes you; not everyone wants the best for you and not everyone wants you to win.

People will talk about you, they will even laugh and boldly tell you to your face that you are wasting time, energy, and resources. This is not always easy to comprehend and many of us have experienced this truth firsthand.

A more comprehensive reason for people not wanting to see you succeed is because if we do, they will begin questioning their own progress in life.

They tend to feel like they are late or that they are not where they should be in life. Therefore, it is easier for them to attempt to press you down, so you do not get further ahead of them.

Sometimes, out of excitement, we want to share our success with our family and friends.

I often do it too, and personally, it is because I want everyone to notice how far I have come because of my hard work. I want them to know that they too can achieve the same outcome – if they do not give up. I want them to understand that dreams can come true. However, as I implied above, not everyone takes kindly to those who want to share or even achieve success.

Yes, some of our friends do not want to see us succeed, despite what they may tell us. It may be hard to determine right away who they are, but what I have noticed is that they always eventually show their ugly faces.

The fourth year comes around and yet the discouraged farmer sees no Chinese bamboo tree; nothing seems to be happening. The farmer begins to wonder:

How much longer can I wait?
How much longer will this take?
Did I make a mistake?
Did I underestimate the time?

The definition of discouragement is when a person has a loss of confidence or enthusiasm.

Honestly, I admit that by this time now, I myself would also be battling with discouragement.

Whenever we as human beings continue to do the right thing but do not have good results, this cannot be easy. We have worked hard, and we have done everything to the best of our human ability, yet there is no sign of what we believed and prayed so hard for.

I believe that we will get discouraged from time to time; this is all a part of life; however, we cannot dwell here. Let us take a closer look at the story of Nehemiah the prophet.

Nehemiah was given the assignment by God to rebuild the walls of Jerusalem. For Nehemiah, this was a burden that he carried day and night; he was desperate to see the walls rebuilt.

Upon arriving at Jerusalem, Nehemiah surveyed the city; he took notice of the damages and put a plan of action in place to begin the process of rebuilding the walls. He gathered everyone together in one place as he spoke to them about what God had put in his heart. Soon, the work was underway.

Nehemiah 4:6 points out that as soon as the people were midway through the building process, they became discouraged.

This is exactly how we are in our daily lives; we start off pursuing new ideas with great excitement and expectations. But the moment things do not happen when and how we perceive that they should happen, we tend to get discouraged.

However, it's at the moment that we are about to receive our breakthrough that the battle intensifies. We look at what we are doing, and it looks like we are making little or no progress at all. It seems like the more we work, the less we accomplish.

If we carefully study this chapter, we can discover the causes and cures for discouragement.

Let me encourage you, do not give up or grow weary when dark times come, for the harder the battle, the sweeter the victory will be.

The more storms you face in life, the stronger you will be. Hold on, the best is ahead of you.

The fifth year comes, and the farmer continues to water, fertilize, and give the seed all the nutrients it needs.........then, finally, spring comes, and little tiny stems begin to develop. ...suddenly within six weeks, the Chinese bamboo tree grows NINETY FEET tall.

Yes! IN only SIX WEEKS!

Isn't life just like the growing process of this Chinese bamboo tree?

First, we set our plans and goals in place; then we complete the vision board.

We do everything that we know will lead us to success, however, we undermine or forget that there is usually a process before we can see the full manifestation of what we are believing God for - our minds begin to tell us that we will never make it in life, or we will never reap the rewards of our labor.

If we want to see God's manifestation in our lives, we must renew our minds. Romans 12:2 - *"Do not be conformed to this world but be transformed by the renewal of your mind. That by testing you may discern what is the will of God, what is good and acceptable and perfect."* -

We must allow the Holy Spirit to work from the inside out and break every stony area of our heart that not only set us back in life, but also can corrupt our mind.

Our lives are likened to that of the Chinese bamboo tree. Deep down inside of all of us, there lies this tree waiting to come forth.

I encourage you to keep watering and believing, and you too will one day be seeing the reward of all your hard work. However, just like the farmer, we must be patient.

Of course, it can be discouraging as we seemingly do things right, and nothing happens. If we continue to do the right things, fasting, praying, showing up, and not allowing discouragement to get the best of us, we will receive the reward of our labor.

Gal 6:7-9 says:

7 Be not deceived; God is not mocked: for whatsoever a man soweth, that shall he also reap.

8 For he that soweth to his flesh shall of the flesh reap corruption; but he that soweth to the Spirit shall of the Spirit reap life everlasting.

9 And let us not be weary in well doing: for in due season we shall reap, if we faint not.

We can learn so much from the process of the Chinese bamboo tree.

The most obvious lesson that can be taught is endurance, determination, faith, and most importantly growth in dark places.

The growth of the Chinese bamboo tree requires the right nutrients, so does our dreams.

At first, we see no visible signs of activity. We apply for the job, and nothing happens, or we fast, we pray, we spend time in the word, only to seemingly get no results.

As time continues to go by, we see no growth; yet again, there are no results. At this point, all our friends are getting married, everyone around us seems to be having children, and we begin to feel left out.

The third and the fourth year goes by and still no manifestation. At this point, we get impatient, our spiritual walk with Christ is tried as we question our efforts, and our ability to hear from God is put to test.

Did God really say that He will bless me?

Did He really say that I would have a worldwide ministry?

Will I ever be rewarded for all my hard work?

Finally, in the fifth year – behold, a miracle!

We see some significant growth. And what a mighty growth it is! The Chinese bamboo tree grows ninety feet in just six weeks.

As I write, I hear the Holy Spirit say that you are about to enter your fifth year. This is the time or season of your life when you will see things manifested.

Those dreams that were hidden are about to suddenly come forth; there is no way that you can contain it any longer!

Despite the way things have looked in the past, or seem in the natural realm, God is introducing many doors of opportunities that were once closed on your behalf.

God is about to do something new in your life. Get ready for your new beginning. God is saying that the glory of the former things cannot compare to the glory of the new thing which is ahead of you. You have the mind of Christ.

His divine power has given you everything that pertains to life and godliness 11 Peter 1:3. You have everything that you need to walk out your divine destiny and fulfill your purpose in life.

God is for you; that battle that you are facing belongs to Him.

You will finish the mandate that He has set before you. Do not grow weary and loose hope.

You will obtain your inheritance.

Perhaps there are some things that you have been praying, believing, and waiting for. Just maybe you are hoping to get married one day, or have a child.

Maybe you are waiting for a relationship to be restored or even healing in your body. Let me remind you that God has an appointed time, and if He makes a promise, you will see it come to pass because He cannot lie.

Numbers 23:19 says: *"God is not a man, that he should lie; neither the son of man, that he should repent: hath he said, and shall he not do it? or hath he spoken, and shall he not make it good?"*

Today, while you are waiting for your appointed time, keep looking for God's favor to follow you. Keep expecting the harvest to be manifested.

Allow God to take you on a journey of growth and development while you are waiting for your appointed time.

Habakkuk 2:3, KJV says: "For the vision is yet for an appointed time, but at the end it shall speak, and not lie: though it tarry, wait for it; because it will surely come, it will not tarry."

Keep praising and worshipping as you wait for the victory. If you are praising and worshipping God, your mind will be focused on Him and all of His promises.

Acts 16:25-26

And at midnight Paul and Silas prayed, and sang praises unto God: and the prisoners heard them. 26: And suddenly there was a great earthquake, so that the foundations of the prison were shaken: and immediately all the doors were opened, and every one's bands were loosed.

As the farmer waits for the Chinese bamboo tree to grow, he had faith that if he kept watering and fertilizing the ground, the tree will appear. You too must have the same kind of faith for your dreams or goals to come through.

This, however, is the hardest part for most of us; we become so anxious about our vision that we simply cannot wait for it to blossom. Then, within days or even months of the planning, we get so discouraged and start to second-guess ourselves or, worse of all, give up.

It is during this dark place in your life you start to wonder if it is worth all the effort, especially when you see others living out their success. Every time you begin to question yourself or allow your emotions to take over, you become double-minded and consumed with self-doubt.

James 1:7-8

7 A double minded man is unstable in all his ways …… For let not that man think that he shall receive any thing of the Lord.

Do not allow yourself to wallow in self-doubt and become double-minded.

If you believe for a second that you have made the wrong decision, ask God to show you how to get your life back on track. Doubt will make you start to think, *"What am I doing trying to grow a Chinese bamboo tree or accomplish a particular dream?"*

Please understand that going after your dream is a definite thing if you just do not give in.

If you keep watering and fertilizing your dream, it will come to fruition, just like the Chinese bamboo tree. It may take weeks. It may take months. It may even take years, but eventually, the roots will take hold and your Chinese bamboo tree will grow.

When it does, it will grow so tall that everyone will see and take note.

Somewhere down on the inside of you, you have a Chinese bamboo tree growing – just waiting to burst through. So, keep watering and believing, and you too will grow so high before you know it.

CHAPTER 2

MY STORY

"Challenges are designed to shape and mold our destiny."

Being the daughter of parents that were preachers and highly esteemed in our community was amazing, however it made me feel pressured to live a life of high expectations.

There was no room for failure in my mind, and this way of thinking caused me to encounter many surprises in my life.

I came from a loving Christian community, a healthy Christian home, and had two older siblings that were not only super protective of me but also extremely supportive. This, however, was not sufficient to keep me from facing some of the greatest challenges I encountered as a young girl.

The pressure that I faced was to perform and live up to people's expectations of how "a young Christian girl" was supposed to live, thus forcing me not to be myself.

Whenever I could not perform to the standards of man, I would isolate myself.

Now that I am an adult, I realized that the greatest gift my parents gave me as a child was taking me to the house of God every single Sunday.

Come rain or sunshine, we were in the house of God to fellowship and worship.

My siblings and I were present at every available worship service during the week; Monday night prayer meeting, Wednesday night bible study, Thursday night youth meeting, and Saturday night choir practice.

Nothing was expected in our home but to pray every day, read the bible, live a God-fearing life, and attend church.

In today's culture, this might seem like a lot, but this upbringing taught me the importance of having a relationship with God.

We not only attended every service, but my parents also made sure we were involved in many of the activities in the church. Because of the involvements in our church, I am blessed with some of the greatest church family, and best friends to this day.

Not only did my parents take us to church, but they also made sure they brought church home to us. Jesus was not just a regular and welcomed guest in our home; He was the center, the circumference, and most importantly, He was the Lord of our home. There were so many nights that my parents read Bible stories and sang the great hymns of old to us before going to bed.

It was no joke when it came time to pray.

I became a Christian at an early age.

As chartered the course for my life and did everything possible to reach every one of my goals, they however were met with many challenges, setbacks, and a great amount of spiritual warfare; Nevertheless, I pressed hard into the things of God with a determination to never give up.

I grew up very sheltered – a life or world that saw everything and everyone through the eyes of love. I was taught to love others as I love myself, do good, and seek peace.

This made me perceived the real world to be the same way. I came to understand later in life that this was not the case; to my surprise, this was not how the real world operated and for a moment, I found it difficult to socially adjust, as I felt like I was too inexperienced in life and for the truth that exists.

This reality had opened my eyes as I experienced various challenges such as pain, rejection, isolation, and feelings of unworthiness. Nobody knew what was going on because I had mastered how not to be open and vulnerable to anybody. I did not want to show my weakness because I was surrounded by people who had a high standard for me, and I did not want them to think otherwise of me.

Life can present us with a series of challenges that come in different shapes and sizes. They sometimes test our patience, our inner strength, and our ability to persevere.

These dark moments in our lives are tough; however, if we consistently mediate on God's Word and spend time in prayer, we can overcome and live our lives successfully.

Personally, I've had my fair share of pain and dark moment. One of them was the loss of my father; the man I considered my greatest pillar of strength, support and joy.

My father taught us so much about practical life and he believed so much in us as every good father would. He was accountable to self and family which made us have a great sense of stability and respect for him.

Every day, we knew where he was, we knew when he was leaving for work and when he would return home from work.

His work was endless, and he never looked for a thank you or any words of affirmation, though those emotions were expressed and shown daily from us.

Although our father loved us so much, he never spoiled us or allowed us to get away with anything. He did not approve of any misdeed or bad behavior. He used tough love to prove his point. His words were very powerful, but they were words of love, wisdom, instructions, and directions.

Just as any other great father knows that his children are mere human beings and can be vulnerable when it comes to making mistakes, so did my father.

He understood that making mistakes was all a part of life. However, this was no excuse to stay or continue toward the wrong paths in life. He made it clear that repeated irresponsible mishaps would not be tolerated.

My father taught us to be appreciative of the small and great things in life.

We were encouraged not to take what we had for granted. From the food on the table and the clothes on our backs, everything was considered a blessing from God.

Growing up on an island where there were not many opportunities for young people, my father encouraged us daily to pursue a good education.

He challenged each one of his children as he led us by example.

He illustrated the importance of love and respect for our mother.

He showed my mother great affection and was never one day shy or afraid to do so in front of his children.

The above description could make you conclude I was my father's pet, maybe I was, but there is another person as wonderful as my father; she is my mom, his one and only wife.

My mother is a godly woman of great faith, she is gentle, sensitive, and very encouraging.

As children and young adults who desperately need the encouragement of their parents, my mother always makes herself available for us.

She always makes us feel valued and loved. By her example, she demonstrates to her children how they too can always love.

Behind every successful man, they say, there is a great woman – my mother was that woman. Her devotion to her husband and children was unparalleled.

She had an unconditional love, and here, is one of the many proofs.

Four years ago, my father (in his late 60s) had gone to bed as usual, only to awaken with his legs numb and unable to walk.

My mother called a family doctor who diagnosed him with a stroke. The stroke made the entire right side of his body unable to move.

It would only be two weeks later after fighting with all his might, to be mobile and independent again, that he suffered another severe stroke. This time, the entire left side of his body was paralyzed. He became completely bedridden.

For the next few weeks, I watched my mother take care of my father with such love and joy. She had to do everything for him and never one day complained.

Exactly two months to the date of his last stroke, my father passed away.

It was the hardest thing I had ever gone through.

I had recently gotten married and miscarried my first son, it was a very dark period for me.

Although I was blessed with a wonderful husband, a supportive family, and great friends that prayed for me, encouraged and counseled me, it could not help the pain of losing my father.

Despite everyone's best intentions, the pain of losing a parent is not something one can properly grasp until they experience it themselves.

To this day, my heart still aches, and I know it always will. But over the years, I have found great solace in the abundant love of my heavenly Father.

Because of His love, I have overcome the spirit of heaviness and grief *(read chapter 4 of this book).*

If you are currently going through a challenging time, you are not alone. As you continue to read through the chapters of this book, I pray that you will find peace as you learn how to overcome the challenges you might be facing right now, or even the challenges that will come your way in the future.

I know that challenges are difficult to overcome. It would not be a challenge if it was easy to overcome, obviously.

Every one of us will go through struggles. Some people will go through more than others, but we all go through difficult times in life.

We cannot escape challenges, but we can choose how we respond to them.

Be reminded of this truth: We have the Greater One living inside of us. The bible says, "For greater is He that is in you - than he that is in the world" (I John 4:4).

Yes, the Greater One lives inside of you!

I Peter 5:8 says: "Be sober, be vigilant; because your adversary, the devil, walketh about, as roaring lion seeking whom he may devour."

The closer you get to God, the more Satan attacks you - because you become a threat to him and his kingdom.

When God has a plan and a purpose for our lives, the enemy would do whatever it takes to distract us. We will face great warfare; life at times will be tough to navigate.

However, adversities are a regular part of our lives as believers.

Our character is developed as we are tested and as we overcome every challenge thrown at us.

The greatest part is that our faith grows as we persevere through life's journey. Even though life's trying obstacles, situations, and calamities show up along the way, we will overcome if we never give up.

Our heavenly Father desires that we make efforts to overcome such trials and difficulties and mature into the women and men that we are meant to be.

We all have unique situations and challenges that will test us. I believe that those trials were tailor-made for us, for our heavenly father knows just how much we can handle. He knows what it takes to bring us into full maturity.

None of us will be placed in a trial without a way out. It is a promise from God: *"No temptation has overtaken you except such as is common to man; but God is faithful, who will not allow you to be tempted beyond what you are able, but with the temptation will also make the way of escape, that you may be able to bear it"* (I Corinthians 10:13).

Nevertheless, such challenges are designed to shape and mold our destiny. It is because of these dark seasons that we grow and develop into the character we are intended to be.

Despite life's challenges, we must keep the faith because it is during these times that we are growing.

Paul was painfully conscious of this, because he had been in adverse circumstances over and over, faced countless trials, and suffered great persecutions:

II Timothy 3:10-11:

"But you have carefully followed my doctrine, manner of life, purpose, faith, longsuffering, love, perseverance, persecutions, afflictions, which happened to me at Antioch, at Iconium, at Lystra—what persecutions I endured. And out of them all the Lord delivered me."

What is most notable about this is that Paul boldly testified about God's ability to deliver us from all that we go through in life - the Lord Himself will deliver us all!

Just like the great pioneers of faith encountered their own obstacles and had to overcome, we must do the same.

The Bible is filled with illustrations of those who overcame great adversities and proved their strength, determination, and character. Let's look at Hannah:

I believe that as a woman, Hannah has one of the most inspiring stories in the Bible. Her life is identifiable today with many women for several reasons.

Hannah was a woman who experienced an overwhelming sorrow. She wanted a child so badly but was unable to bear one because she was barren. She cried out to God that He should give her a son and in return, she promised to dedicate his life back to God for service.

God heard Hannah's prayer and granted her a son, and she named him Samuel. Hannah lived up to her promise; as soon as her son was old enough, she took him to be raised in the temple.

Today, Hannah is also recognized for her great sacrifice; she dedicated her baby boy Samuel to the Lord and saw to it that he served God "all the days of his life" (1 Samuel 1:11).

Samuel later grew up to be one of the most powerful and God-fearing men in the Bible. One of the greatest testimonies about Hannah's life is that she never gave up hope that God would hear and answer her prayer.

Jesus said in John 15:4-5: "Abide in Me, and I in you. As the branch cannot bear fruit of itself, unless it abides in the vine, neither can you, unless you abide in Me. I am the vine; you are the branches. He who abides in Me, and I in him, bears much fruit; for without Me you can do nothing."

Every encounter we effectively conquer with the grace and aid of the Holy Spirit, helps to strengthen our confidence and our ability to face future obstacles, as it helps to shape our purpose and our faith.

The Word of God declares: *"For everyone to whom much is given, from him much will be required; and to whom much has been committed, of him they will ask the more."*

But we now have Him as our Advocate and Helper. It is vitally important that we stay connected with the Vine, our source of power, and growth.

Paul writes to encourage us from *Romans 8:37: "Yet in all these things we are more than conquerors through Him who loved us".*

Therefore, as we walk our daily walk, we must persevere, overcome, and conquer the adverse challenges arrayed against us. This is how we build the faith and character that our great God desires to see in us, the faith and character of our Savior Jesus Christ.

Remember, as Jesus was sent to fulfill His mission here on earth, He was met with great challenges. He had to deal directly with Satan himself.

Jesus was challenged so many times by those who wished to kill Him.

Just as He had to face challenges, and overcame we as His followers will have to face challenges and overcome.

When my firstborn son (Jaydon) was a bit younger, he would always sleep in the room with my husband and I. However, as he got older, we moved him to his very own room so that he could begin sleeping in his own bed; however, somewhere around 2:00 a.m. every morning, we would hear him crying at our bedside.

Whenever Jaydon woke up and realized that he was alone in his dark room, he got afraid. But as he cuddled up next to us, he would sleep perfectly fine.

This, however, is so true for some of us; often, it is the problems in life we face and the fact that we think we are facing them alone that scares us so much.

Psalms 23:4 – "Yea, though I walk through the valley of the shadow of death, I will fear no evil: for thou art with me; thy rod and thy staff they comfort me."

Moreover, the truth we must hold fast to is that, even in the darkest night, when we go through our most difficult seasons, we are never alone: our heavenly Father is always with us.

While teaching His disciples, Jesus' final Words before He ascended to heaven were: *"I am with you always, even to the end of the age." (Matthew 28:20)*

God is always with us – we are never alone.

God longs for us to know His love, grace, and mercy will forever be available to us. He longs to have sweet fellowship and communion with us. God desires nothing more than to mend our broken hearts. Every secret prayer that you have prayed and hoped for in life, God wants to give to you.

John 10:10: "I have come so that you may have life in all its fullness."

Isaiah 41: 10: So, do not fear, for I am with you; do not be dismayed, for I am your God. I will strengthen you and help you; I will uphold you with my righteous right hand."

As you read and meditate on the words in this book, I want to encourage you, right now to allow its words to penetrate deep into your heart.

Isaiah 43:1-3:

"The Lord who created you says, 'Do not be afraid – I will save you. I have called you by name you are mine. When you pass through deep waters, I will be with you; your troubles will not overwhelm you. When you pass through fire, you will not be burnt; the hard trials that come will not hurt you. For I am the Lord your God, the holy God of Israel who saves you…You are precious to me. Do not be afraid – I am with you!"

CHAPTER 3

MULTIPLE MISCARRIAGES

Setting the course for my life- my life is not my own

I am the youngest of three, and because of that, I stayed home with my parents much longer. I was always very close to my parents; I loved my father so much, but I emulated my mother. I watched the way that she cared for all the neighbors' children and loved them as her own.

My mother raised so many other children right in our home. Seeing her love and patience for my siblings and I, and the other children in the various communities of Grand Bahama, made me realize that I was destined to be a mom myself.

I would always wonder, "could I be as great a mother as she is". I did not think so, but I was willing to try.

My husband and got married in 2016, and by the second month of our marriage I was pregnant.

I remember going to my parents' house and literally begging my mom to make a special dish. I just had to have some fried chicken and it had to be prepared immediately.

My mom looked at me and laughed, she realized that something was different about me, but she kept her thoughts to herself. She eagerly waited for me to confirm to her what I did not know at the time; that I was pregnant.

Within that week, I found out that I was pregnant. I was so excited; I was overcome with exceeding joy! My greatest dream was about to come true!

As I saw the little life that was on the screen of the ultrasound and heard its precious heartbeat in my doctor's office, everything just seemed so surreal.

We just knew that we had created something special and beautiful and it was living and growing on the inside of me. My husband became super protective of his seed inside of me. We were completely over the moon.

We shared the good news with everyone we met; we were just happy. Family and friends began to congratulate us. They would always ask the famous question, "Do you want a boy or a girl?"

My response was always the same, "I really don't care, as long he/she is well."

Weeks had passed, and our baby kept growing and developing. Months had passed and we found out the sex; it was a baby boy! We named him Joshua.

One day, exactly five months into that pregnancy, I was using the bathroom, and suddenly, I spotted blood. It was heavy and a bit abnormal.

My husband immediately took me to the emergency room; there, we found out that the baby was coming. My body then went into premature labor.

Within two days of lying in the hospital hoping and praying that my body would be strong enough to carry baby Joshua to full term, he came.

It was Mother's Day 2016 that I pushed out my greatest dream – my first baby boy - but unfortunately, he was dead! I just remembered feeling like someone had thrown me into a deep dark pit and deliberately began pouring brick on me one by one. It was as if my entire world was just crashing in. Every minute that went by was harder than the last. I was just devastated.

My husband and I showed our grief in different ways. (I later learned that this was quite normal). He wanted to hear more official news from the doctors. He wanted to know what happened and how we could prevent this from happening again.

He was processing his pain in a far different way than me; however, because he was grieving in a different way, it did not mean the loss hurt him any less.

This made me feel overwhelmed and that I was all alone.

After the miscarriage, I cried day and night. I had no desire to get out of bed, and just like many other women, I blamed myself.

The loss of our first child really hurt us both.

Although we were faced with so many uncertainties, we were determined not to give up.

It would be seven months later to the time of losing my first baby that I was pregnant again. This time around, we were sure to do everything right as we were more prepared.

This pregnancy was relatively ordinary; I stayed off my feet for the most part. We decided that I would not work throughout this pregnancy. I experienced severe morning sickness. According to my doctors this was good, as it was a great indication that the baby was growing well. I was mindful to take my vitamins and I tried my best to eat healthy. There were some foods and drinks I gave up like coffee and food with too much salt. I tried to do everything right and was looking forward to having a healthy, successful birth.

Three months into this pregnancy, we found out that we would be having a baby girl. I was so afraid, but so very excited at the same time.

We quickly selected a name; we called her baby Jeniah. I prayed for her daily as I called her by her name while still in my womb. Already, we had a great bond.

Everything was wonderful, all my doctor's appointments went well and there was no sign of defects. This was my second pregnancy; I was so happy about it. I had tried so hard to keep everything as smooth as possible.

Two months later, things started to feel different. Again, I was just five months into the pregnancy. One night while having dinner, I felt an urge to use the restroom. To my surprise, I spotted blood. Knowing what I had already gone through, I immediately told my husband to take me to the hospital.

Driving to the hospital, I felt so uneasy. I knew something was happening to my body. I was very worried and so afraid.

Upon my arrival at the hospital, I was rushed through to the emergency room and was asked several questions because of my previous miscarriages. I had no idea what was happening - finding out only minutes later that I was in premature labor AGAIN. Lord have mercy!

Immediately, the doctor began calling some of the high-risk hospitals to see if a bed was available for me. After only minutes of calling the top hospitals, I was transported via ambulance to deliver my baby.

Everything happened so fast; the doctors were so professional; they did everything they possibly could to ensure that the baby lived.

I was given the option for steroid injections to help strengthen and prepare my baby's lungs for breathing outside the womb. Of course, I agreed to it, as I was willing to do anything for my daughter to live. Shortly after, the nurses came inside my room and injected me with the steroids.

The next day, I gave birth to my baby girl. She was so tiny but so beautiful. Baby Jeniah had weighed a little over one pound. I sat beside her incubator night and day. Going home to rest or shower was never an option.

After eight days of fighting for life, my precious baby girl died. Baby Jeniah was too young and too tiny to fight off an infection she had caught.

At this point, I was so sure that my world was over! When my baby died, a great part of me died as well. I knew that I could never, in a million years, be the same.

As my baby girl was dying, I held her in my arms and began to sing:

> *"Tis so sweet to trust in Jesus,*
> *Just to take Him at His Word*
> *Just to rest upon His promise,*
> *Just to know, "Thus saith the Lord!"*
> *Jesus, Jesus, how I trust Him!*
> *How I've proved Him o'er and o'er*
> *Jesus, Jesus, precious Jesus!*
> *Oh, for grace to trust Him more"*

With my husband, the doctors, and nurses all around me, I held my dying baby up and said, "God, I thank you for the eight days that you allowed me to be a mother. I thank You for the life of Jeniah. She has taught me so much. She taught me how to fight to the end. I will never forget that!"

I walked away from that hospital room feeling so empty. The depth of the pain that I was carrying could not be described.

For the next few days, I found myself preparing for my very own daughter's burial. I had to arrange how to transport her body from the hospital to the funeral home. Also, I had to decide the color of the dress that she would wear and the design of her little casket.

One might ask or even wonder how I was able to do all of this. The only answer that I can give is that had it not been for the Lord on my side, I know that I would not have made it. I felt like a failure; I felt like I had failed as a mother. The guilt that I felt was terrible.

There were days that I thought that I was responsible in some way for my baby not being alive. I questioned all the things I had done over the last few months and wondered if there was something, I had done to cause my baby's brief life on earth to end.

Although I was doing my best to encourage others, I was struggling with so much hurt.

Prior to having baby Jeniah, I was scheduled to preach during Sunday morning service. When I came out of the hospital, my Pastor asked if I would still be able to preach during Sunday morning service, and I said yes.

Romans 8:28: "And we know that all things work together for the good to those that love the Lord and are called to his purpose."

The title of the message was, "There Is Purpose for Your Pain." As I stood before the congregation, I began to preach and share with them my experience, and where I was, and how I felt. At the time, the Holy Spirit took over and began speaking through me. I shared with the congregation that despite what anyone is going through, there is a purpose for their pain.

At that moment, I did not even understand what I was preaching, or what I was saying, but I knew that I was being led by the Holy Spirit.

It was one year later that I really began to understand that there was indeed purpose for my pain (read chapter five of this book).

I was hurting so badly, I had just gone through trauma, but I realized that God was using my story to bring strength to those who were hurting as well. There was not a dry eye in the congregation as I declared the word of God.

Six months after losing baby Jeniah, I was pregnant again. Everything was going great with this pregnancy, as it always did in the beginning.

Exactly twenty-one weeks pregnant, I woke up excited about my doctor's appointment. My excitement was beyond my control as I saw my baby's heart beating on the ultrasound. I noticed the technician leave the room and came back with a doctor. I was instantly gripped with fear when the emergency doctor told me that my cervix was a bit shorter than normal and that the best thing for me was to go on complete bed rest.

Because of my history, I was sent home to pack my bags and return to the hospital the very next day. They admitted me to the hospital immediately.

That next day, I met with the high-risk team of doctors. I had a thorough ultrasound that confirmed what was seen before. My baby looked wonderful on the screen, which was encouraging. I was prepared to do whatever it took to save this baby, even if it meant that I had to spend the rest of my pregnancy in the hospital. I was told that there was a one hundred percent chance that the baby would come early, and it was important that I stayed as close to the hospital as possible if this happens.

Weeks came and passed; my body was doing great and so was my growing baby. Every doctor's visit was filled with so many emotions. I was so afraid of losing another baby.

I disliked being in the hospital, I was lonely, as I was away from my husband and my family for so long. I was worried about my body ever being able to provide a safe home for my unborn baby, but I trusted God.

I finally accepted that I had no control over the situation. I cried out to God day and night. I confessed the scriptures over my body and the baby. I confessed these scriptures and got them deep down in my heart. The more I knew God's will concerning my unborn child, the more I grew in my faith that everything would be ok. I began to boldly speak out God's Word, and patiently await its manifestation. I meditated on the scriptures below until they all became a part of me.

Scriptures:

- He gives the childless woman a family, making her a happy mother. Praise the LORD! Psalm 113:9

- I prayed for this child, and the LORD has granted me what I asked of him. 1 Samuel 1:27 Hannah's prayers for a child were answered.

- For the LORD God is our sun and our shield. He gives us grace and glory. The LORD will withhold no good thing from those who do what is right. Psalm 84:11

- *Lo, children [are] an heritage of the LORD: [and] the fruit of the womb [is his] reward. As arrows [are] in the hand of a mighty man; so [are] children of the youth. Happy [is] the man that hath his quiver full of them: they shall not be ashamed, but they shall speak with the enemies in the gate. Psalms 127:3, 4, 5*

I shed many tears, but despite all of this I was growing so much closer to God.

My faith and confidence in Him began to grow. I knew that being in the hospital was the safest thing for me and my baby, but I did not realize that this time alone was ordained by God.

As a result of this time spent in the hospital, my relationship with God grew deeper, closer and, even stronger through spending time alone with Him.

This time alone with God was so important as He began to purge and transform me. I came out of that hospital knowing God in a way that I never knew Him before. I experienced a new level of freedom to express myself to Him as I allowed Him to speak directly to my heart through His Word and through prayer.

God is the source of our strength, and when we spend time in the presence of God, in prayer and in meditation on His Word, we are moving mountains that we might not even be able to see.

After almost four months of being admitted to the hospital in order to prolong my pregnancy and carry the baby to full term, I was finally released. It was a celebration in the making as I was discharged from Mt. Saini Hospital, being eight months pregnant. I had never gone that long in any of my pregnancies and doctors were certain that if anything was to happen the baby would be fine. I was so happy to be back in the comfort of my own home.

Days of being home turned into weeks, and I was still very much pregnant.

Just weeks later, on June 7th I went to the hospital at 8:30 p.m. because of contraction.

I was examined by the doctor and was already six centimeters dilated.

Immediately, I was admitted to the hospital, and by 6:30 a.m. on June 8th, I gave birth to the most handsome, full haired (matured) baby boy weighing 8 pounds.

The doctor placed his naked body across my chest. I gazed at his face, his feet, his tiny fingers, and saw that everything was so perfect. I stared at him and kissed his little forehead.

He was more than I could have ever dreamt that he would be. He had a head full of hair and his skin was very soft. He looked so precious and peaceful as he opened his eyes and looked up at me. At that moment, I realized everything I had gone through was entirely worth it, and if I had too, I would do it again in a heartbeat.

For the first time I would be walking out of the hospital with a baby in my arms and not feeling empty, or as if I had failed.

God will do it AGAIN and AGAIN

After the loss of multiple pregnancies and overcoming the pain and trauma that accompanied each lost, my faith in God grow tremendously.

I was now a mother of a healthy baby boy named Jaydon.

However, God decided that He would do it again.

Eight months after having Jaydon, I was pregnant again.

This pregnancy was much different than the others, I was less afraid and more confident in God's ability to complete what he had started in me.

This pregnancy not only confirmed that God had indeed healed my body, but it confirmed how much I had grown in my level of faith.

I carried this baby straight through to full term with absolutely no complications.

On November 14th, 2019, I gave birth to my second son, we named him Josiah.

The name JOSIAH mean Jehovah has healed.

God not only healed me physically, but he healed me emotionally.

God blessed me with two healthy beautiful boys and a wonderful stepson.

I am the proud mother of three handsome boys. God is so good, and His mercies endure forever.

He has changed my story. It does not matter how difficult your situation might seem, with God all things are possible, and things can change for the best in your life.

CHAPTER 4

OVERCOMING GRIEF

Within months apart, I lost my first pregnancy and the closest human being to me on the face of the earth (my father).

The passing of a loved one is inevitable; however, it is still difficult to accept any loss, especially the loss of a parent.

My father's passing was not easy to understand; one day, he was perfectly fine, then within just a few months, he would no longer be with us.

The death of a parent can be filled with grief, shock, and it can forever change families, because it entails that a bond is forcefully broken. In most cases, nothing is ever the same again.

Losing both my father and my first pregnancy within weeks apart was traumatic.

I experienced severe grief.

The bond between my father and I was very strong. I wanted to be just like him.

Because I had such a great relationship with my father, I am blessed to be able to look back at all the warm memories I had with him when growing up.

My primary love languages were quality time, and my father was big on spending time with his family. He would normally take this time and listen to me as a child and as an adult; it was so easy to communicate with him. He always showed us unconditional love. My father was a great protector to his family. No matter what, he stood with us and he stood up for us.

There were so many great qualities my father had; however, the one quality that had the greatest effect on me was his willingness to understand his children. I cannot recall a day he got upset at me or my siblings for our faults or failures. However, he encouraged us to do better and always to give our best.

As a young lady, I felt so secure because of the love I received from him. This sense of security is very important for a daughter as she develops and matures in life, because it gives the support for her to flourish in a rather safe atmosphere if she has the confidence in knowing that her father would always be there for her. Because I came from such an environment, I developed self-confidence at an early age.

Having such an upright relationship with my father did not only shape my childhood experience, but also it influenced my conduct towards others later in life. All these traits shaped the way in which I perceived my heavenly Father.

Because of my earthly father's love for me, I can view and express my love towards my heavenly Father in a greater way. This song by Christ Tomblin depicts every emotion I feel towards a loving heavenly Father:

"This I've heard a thousand stories of what they think you're like
But I've heard the tender whispers of love in the dead of night
And you tell me that you're pleased
And that I'm never alone
You're a good good father
It's who you are, it's who you are, it's who you are
And I'm loved by you
It's who I am, it's who I am, it's who I am"

The love and bond between my father and I were undeniably great; therefore, watching him in his final days of life knowing there was literally nothing I could do to make the situation better was extremely hard. I realized that it was the little things that I did that mattered the most to him – like just keeping him company as often as possible.

Can you imagine the pain and frustration we faced knowing there was nothing that we could do to ease the pain of the one we loved so much?

Almost every day for almost six months, this was our reality.

Despite the pain, my father would preach and encourage everyone around him. His faith was stronger than ours; his personality was stronger than ours; his upbringing was stronger than ours.

I remember two messages saying, "This too shall pass" and "My comeback is greater than this setback!" He was our greatest strength during his most difficult days of life. He remained positive and did everything to be grateful for life.

Every day of his life, during the last four months, it became harder and harder as we endured the ineffable pain of watching him unable to move as he wished.

My mother was and is a prayer warrior from the time that I can remember. Her life and actions towards my father taught me, as a wife, how to treat and care for my husband.

My mother cared for my father better than any nurse or doctor could have done. For my mom, it was a pleasure to serve and take care of my father and she did so until he passed on.

She personified the persona of a Proverbs 31 woman:

Proverbs 31:11-12: "Her husband has full confidence in her and lacks nothing of value. She brings him good, not harm, all the days of her life."

Proverbs 31:25: "She is clothed with strength and dignity; she can laugh at the days to come."

Just like my family, if you have taken care of a loved one, even for a brief period, you would be able to empathize with the indescribable, arduous sense of seeing them bear such pain.

I was with my father every step of the way while in therapy, to hospital appointments and ambulance calls. It was emotionally stressful to see him so helpless, but it was an honor to take care of him as he had done so for me all my life.

The emotions I felt during his illness lingered for a very long time. There was nothing that I could do to get rid of that pain. I would often hold my father's hands and whisper a prayer in silence for the pain to subside. I felt so powerless, as I had to accept that I was not in control.

"Death leaves a heartache no one can heal; love leaves a memory no one can steal." From an Irish headstone." Everyone has a hero in their lifetime; as for me, my hero was my father. He was always present if I needed his help, support, or wise counsel. I would never forget the distressing phone call I got from my mom while I was at work one morning.

Unexpectedly, my father's condition had worsened, and he was no longer responding, my mother called the family immediately.

Meanwhile, I had just seen my father the night before and he looked so hopeful.

As the family gathered around his bedside, he smiled and looked so peaceful. However, within an hour or less, my father was gone. He was taken from time into eternity, just as he preached about all his life.

Everyone cried as we gave thanks to God for the life he lived and the service that he had rendered.

My father was a dad to many and a man of great influence in our community. There was never a day that I can recall that our home was not filled with family and friends bringing gifts and stopping by to show love and support.

I can remember crying all through the night. I didn't sleep, as I turned and tossed that night in agony. I felt so empty; there was a pain in my chest that I could not explain. I was in shock for days; I was not prepared for this at all. I had no clue that the feeling of losing my father would be so unbearable.

As the days and weeks went by, I didn't do much but cry.

Grief is the response to losing something or someone, particularly where there was a great bond or affection formed. Grieving is a natural part of life; loss happens to all of us and it is expressed differently in different cultures.

We will all experience grief one day, whether it's a parent, friend, or coworker. Grief does not always come in the form of the death of someone; you can have an emotional response regarding any loss. And, certainly, as people lose their jobs and even go in and out of relationships, they are experiencing grief.

1 Thessalonians 4 verse 13:

But we do not want you to be uninformed brothers about those who are asleep by asleep he means who have died, that you may not grieve as others do who have no hope. How interesting. He says, this uninformed the literal word here is I don't want you to be ignorant.

Grief is one of the hardest emotional strains in life. It's a gnawing pain that can make one feel empty as they try to cope with the loss of something or someone, they hold close to them.

My father was my entire world, he was the glue that held our family together.

I remember a close friend who also happens to be a psychologist, praying with me through this very difficult time in my life.

She explained the different stages of grief which comes in the form of depression, anger, acceptance, denial and isolation. She assured me that it will definitely take time to get over such loss.

I did not necessarily go through all these stages, but I did live in denial and I isolated myself for a very long time.

Everyone grieves and mourns at the experience of a great loss; however, we all show grief differently.

My father's death inspired me to evaluate my life and my service to God's kingdom. I finally gained an understanding of life, and that we are here on earth for only a short while.

I would hear my father saying, "*Nacquel, as long as there is life, there is hope and as long as there is hope, there is life. Keep living and working for the Master, the greatest reward one can receive is eternal life.*"

Months later, grief continued gnawing at me night and day; it felt as if the pain would never go away.

I began praying for divine intervention. I reflected on the great times I had with my father and the lessons he taught me. I was assured of one thing and that is, my father would not want to see me so depressed and hopeless over his death as I had become.

After my father's death, the reality of his burial set in. We began preparing for the funeral. We picked out the clothes that he would wear. We choose the funeral home. We met with the directors to go over the obituary. This all felt so surreal, could this really be happening? Why were we referring to my father in past tense?

We talked about the life that my father lived, the photos and everything. Throughout this process, I did my best to remain calm. The peace of God, which surpasses all understanding, remained with us as we prepared for the funeral. However, the reality of my father's death set in after the funeral. So many unanswered questions. The feeling of guilt – could I have done anything differently, like pray harder or maybe fast longer? Every emotion one could imagine attacked my mind. Everything in my life, or every area in my life, was affected by his loss.

As a result of my father's death, I felt lost. I did not know where to turn or how I would make it through. I felt empty; something was missing; in fact, it felt like a big part of me was missing. My first love, my protector, my provider, my wisdom guy was missing.

Some days, the weight of depression was so heavy. There were days where I just would lie in bed, sleep, and not go to work. As I walked through our home, everything reminded me of my dad. From the clothes in the closet to the car parked in the driveway, the keys still in place. The sight of his obituary on the table felt so surreal. It just wasn't right; it wasn't supposed to happen like this. Not to him, not right now. He was so young, he was so vibrant, you know, there was not much preparation. There were no goodbyes.

Somehow, I was angry and bitter, and I did not want to be around anyone. I would isolate myself. I was experiencing far too much loss. One night, I cried out to God from the debts of my very being to take the pain away. It was far more than I could bear.

To escape what I was going through, I decided to go on vacation.

We traveled to Toronto, Ontario. While I was staying in my hotel room, a lady mistakenly knocked on my door. She was looking for someone else; however, she invited me to a revival service that would be happening that very night in the conference room of the same hotel. Reluctantly, I decided to go because she was so nice to me.

As I sat in the last row of that revival service and listened to the old gospel hymns being sang, I felt a peaceful presence. The choir along with the congregants sang the song "*On Christ the Solid Rock I stand, all other ground is sinking sand.*" This was my father's favorite song! I wept like a baby.

The minister preached a powerful sermon, and by the look on so many faces, deliverance was taking place. After he was finished preaching, he called me out and asked if it was ok to pray with me. I said yes; at this point, I had nothing to lose.

As he laid hands on me and prayed for me, he prayed that the spirit of heaviness would leave. I remember lying on the floor weeping and worshipping God, and when I got up to return to my seat, I felt so different. It was one of the most peaceful moments I had experienced since losing my father. I felt so light, and for the first time in a long time I was happy; I had joy unspeakable. The feeling like bags of rocks on my shoulders that weighed so many pounds each, were removed.

That night my life was changed forever. It was so much easier to sit and talk about my father's life with my siblings. We talked about happy memories and the good times we had growing up. We also talked about the life lessons that we learnt.

The most fun I had with my father was sitting outside on our veranda, watching cars drive by and greeting the neighbors as they walked by.

I could remember my father planting fruits and vegetables in our backyard, harvesting them, and gladly preparing them for our family. I loved the sugarcane so much; the way that he took his time to peel it and cut it up in chunks was done as a gesture of love.

There were days when we decided to go on diets together. We also and walked the block of our neighborhood together for hours. We would drive to the beach and talk for long periods.

One of the greatest lessons he taught me was to appreciate everything, do not regret anything, because in life there are many lessons to learn from everything.

Even if the path takes you to a dead end, remember that the journey will be worth taking.

As hard as this process was to accept, I turned to the word of God daily for strength and comfort. Every day, I would quote scriptures like:

Revelation 21:4: 'He will wipe every tear from their eyes. There will be no more death' or mourning or crying or pain...'

Psalm 34:18: 'The LORD is close to the brokenhearted and saves those who are crushed in spirit.'

John 8:36: ' If the Son therefore shall make you free, ye shall be free indeed.'

Psalm 147:3:' He heals the brokenhearted and binds up their wounds.'

Romans 8:28: 'And we know that in all things God works for the good of those who love him, who have been called according to his purpose.'

As I meditated on God's word, I found comfort and strength. Even though the pain was still present, it was not as painful.

CHAPTER 5

A GREATER CAUSE FOR OUR PAIN

"Why does God allow pain and suffering, when He is all powerful and can prevent it?"

This is one of the questions people have asked for centuries.

When we go through painful situations in our lives, one of the reasons that God allows it is so that His glory can be revealed.

Pain draws us to God and pain reveals who we are. I believe that anything that draws us to God is worth it. Whether we like it or not. We will also discover the awesome power of God to comfort and sustain us in difficult times

It is one thing to rejoice and be exceedingly happy when things are going our way. However, how do we respond when we are not feeling well?

How do we respond when we are restricted?

There are some things we learn during suffering and pain, that we will not learn any other way.

As I look back over time, I realize that the miscarriages, the grief, the financial hardships, and the times of the greatest suffering that I have been through, were preparing me for this very moment; the moment in which I would have the opportunity to share my life experience as a leader to help other people who are going through the same thing.

"No one is exempt from the trials of life, but everyone can always find something positive in everything; even in the worst of times."

— Roy T. Bennett

Always Remember! God has a purpose and He also has a plan. He will turn things around for our good; if our response is thanksgiving and a heart of praise, although we do not always understand or even feel up to it. God wants us to trust Him...

"Trust and obey,
For there's no other way
To be happy in Jesus,
But to trust and obey.
Not a burden we bear,
Not a sorrow we share,
But our toil He doth richly repay;
Not a grief or a loss,
Not a frown or a cross,
But is blest if we trust and obey"

I know it is hard to trust God when it seems like everything is going wrong - when we cannot afford school fees and our dreams of graduation must be on held.

Sometimes it seems like we are not moving forward in life – we are going under. We are tempted to live our lives feeling overwhelmed and frustrated with all that is going on. But we must trust God, even when we cannot understand everything that is happening.

God's ways are not our way; He can see things that we cannot see. He knows what we do not know.

Sometimes life might not seem fair, but that does not mean that God is not in full control. I know that your steps are being ordered by Him and that He is allowing things to happen in order to perfect you. It may not feel good now; yes, things really look bad and you are uncomfortable, but when it all comes together, you will see how everything has worked to your advantage.

That problemed child - that difficult marriage - the delay or the betrayal are all helpful in you reaching your purpose Without such difficulty, you would not become who you were created to be.

Everything might seem like a major challenge now, but God is setting you up for a promotion. Every closed door is closed so that a bigger door can open for you. Do you believe it?

Trust Him!

God sometimes moves people out of our way so He can bring real, lasting, meaningful relationships in your life. It hurts so badly sometimes, but what you cannot see is that you are growing; your character is being developed; you are getting stronger and wiser; your confidence is growing; your determination is being increased.

God is still in control of your live.

The steps of a good man are ordered by Him; trust Him to chart the course for your life and the lives of your children and family.

Although you cannot see it or even feel it right at this moment, behind the scenes, God is lining up things in your favor.

I believe that in life we miss out on some great lessons when we only focus on the pain that we go through rather than on God's divine purpose.

If we can see and understand the purpose behind the pain, we can navigate through life in a better way. Difficult times in life can develop our faith and the faith of people around us.

We must understand that pain is inevitable - difficult moments are coming in your life. Just because we are believers or followers of Jesus, we are not exempt from this.

Pain is a vehicle that gets you to your destiny. Jesus said to His disciples in

St John 16:32, *"In this world, you will have trouble: but be of good cheer; I have overcome the world."*

The apostle Paul said in Acts 14:22, *"Through much tribulation, we will enter the kingdom."*

Although it is hard, I want you to celebrate when you are surrounded by a variety of painful situations, with various shades of aggravations and setbacks.

We can celebrate when difficult situations surround us because we know that they carry the potential within them that God can use to mature us. We can be assured that in our problems, God has a purpose! Something positive can be produced by our pain.

Under God's sovereign care, our pain has a purpose, therefore, we can praise God rightfully amid our problems because we know He has a purpose in every one of our pains. God will put you in a difficult moment, but it's not to break you down; it is actually to build strength in you so that you can endure trying times.

When it comes to the trials of life, sometimes the way we overcome is to simply, humbly, and faithfully endure.

Nothing testifies to the pure, faithful reality of God's presence in the life of a believer like observing a believer keep his eyes on Jesus while going through hell on earth.

Seeing believers remain steadfast and seek the face of God in setbacks, hurt, and anger, while keeping the faith, is perhaps the greatest testimony of their life.

Our response to suffering has the power to change those who are watching us when we do not even know it. Everyone will go through trials in life. The only question is, "How do we respond to life's trials?"

My father always taught us that the best way to respond to trials is to rejoice. He also taught us that trials are common to all mankind. One thing is for certain, most people have either just gone through a trial, is in a trial or they are getting ready to encounter one.

Let us face it, we cannot change most of the circumstances in our lives; however, we can change how we respond to them. We need the grace of God every day to help us overcome.

James 1:12 says, *"Blessed is the man who remains steadfast under trial, for when he has stood the test, he will receive the crown of life, which God has promised to those who love him."*

Knowing that we have a crown of life waiting for us after this life or at Jesus' appearance, should give us great joy.

Situations will come and go, but God will provide a way out for us. Sometimes it might not happen right away, but we can still *".... rejoice in our sufferings, knowing that suffering produces endurance" (Rom 5:3).*

Believe me, these things might be a curveball to us, but to God, they are all within His sovereign work in our lives. Everything that happens has a reason and a purpose for it.

There are times when I questioned my process. I wondered, *"What in the world is going on with my life?*

What did I do wrong?
Why do I find myself going through the same challenges again?
When will I finally get what I have been praying for, for so long?
Why, God, why?
How God, how?
When, God, when?"

What I have discovered is that God loves us, and He has a great plan for our lives; however, no one promised us that would be easy. We all will go through difficult times and things will happen that is not fair to us. No doubt, some of the hardships we might be facing is a result of our own disobedience; however, God's love toward us is everlasting. He is merciful and full of compassion.

We should not get confused and lose our faith in Him when life gets hard, because God always causes things to work out for our good.

Thankfully, the word of God says, *"But be of good cheer and take courage; be confident, certain, undaunted! For I (Jesus) have overcome the world."* This is such a great assurance that if we are followers of Christ, everything is going to work out for us the way that it should, in the end.

There were days that I hurt so badly; I did not know how much longer I would be able to bear the weight of what I was carrying. I had to remember that *"His yoke is easy, and His burden is light." Matt 11:30.*

There were times when I did not understand why God would allow me to go through some of the things I have been through.

I remember praying many times for God to rescue me from painful situations. I had to learn from the overwhelming situations I was going through how to trust God when I did not understand and how to release my faith during the trials.

God wanted me to come to the place in my walk with Him where I trusted His sovereignty and understand that He was in control of my life.

God only wants the best for us. He has our best interest at heart even when our circumstances do not seem fair. God wants us to rest in Him and have His peace that surpasses all human understanding, in every situation we encounter.

CHAPTER 6

PUSHING PAST YOUR PAIN (NEVER GIVE UP)

Gaining Endurance - Character

Romans 5:3-4 – Perseverance Produces Character. ...

We often find ourselves stuck at the halfway mark of reaching our goals and wanting to quit. Sometimes we invest so much in our personal development and growth. Whatever it is that we are trying to obtain, we must rely fully on the Holy Spirit and give it everything we have got.

Whether it is improving your marriage, getting out of debt, or running a marathon - whatever it is, you must write your vision down and go after it.

We should never try to avoid discomfort by any means.

One thing you must understand is that difficulties, struggles and the ability to push through are all a part of life; you are only gaining spiritual muscles. The more you push through difficult situations and refuse to give up, the bigger your muscle grows. One day, you will get to the point where you are so used to pushing through situations that it becomes a good healthy habit.

This is when you will start to accomplish great things.

If you were never tempted to overcome obstacles or to quit, you would never really understand that through Christ, you can do all things.

If you are determined to achieve great things, you cannot give in to the resistance; just keep fighting every day.

If you continue to fight that battle and keep pushing, you will start to realize that you will rise above everyone around you. You will start achieving things you never thought that you were capable of. This is a battle that you will fight for the rest of your life.

As you study the Word of God and spend time in His presence, the better prepared you will be for fighting all the adversities that will be thrown at you in the future.

Everyone loves a great success story and will love the manifestation or the transformation.

Everyone anticipates a script where the main character completely messes up, then they fight to get it together again.

One day, you will look back, and realize it was all worth it; it was worth the pain you suffered, the difficulty you faced.

The attitude you have when facing struggles and obstacles is what determines your outcome. Your attitude is everything. Being able to keep moving forward despite the adversity thrown at you is the key.

If you fail, again and again, keep pushing! You argue with your friends or your spouses, keep pushing! Your finances are limited and bills are due, keep pushing! Keep on pushing through the pain, chaos, frustration, disappointment, etc.

Keep pushing through it all! Have the mindset that if you did it once, you can do it again, and each time after that, it gets easier and easier.

The more you overcome your struggles today, the easier you'll overcome your struggles tomorrow, and once you build up that momentum of improving your endurance, it becomes a whole lot easier.

If you fight off the distractions and truly focus on the prize consistently, you will start to see results.

There might not be a sudden manifestation or a quick fix; however, it is an accumulation of staying focused night and day and pushing through your painful circumstances that moves you higher in God.

In this life, you are going to face a lot of disappointments, failures, pains, setbacks, and defeats.

You will discover some things about yourself that you might not know right now; however, always remember that you have greatness within you!

What you will realize is that you' are more powerful than you can ever begin to imagine. However, be reminded that it is not only important that you believe and begin to know that it is possible for you to overcome your pain, but also, it is necessary that you allow the Holy Spirit to work on you, that you allow Him to develop you.

It is important that you stay grounded in the word of God and remove negative people that can drain you emotionally and spiritually.

Get the energy drainers and the dream killers out of your life. These are people who do not want you to progress.

You are going to laugh again. You are going to love again. You are going to dream again. You are going to lead again. You are getting up again. God will turn your mourning into dancing. He will take away your sadness and pain.

God is going to make up for the losses. He is going to reward you for the sorrow, the hurt, and the injustices;

I encourage you to keep your hopes up.

CHAPTER 7

YOU ARE GROWING

Pain is inevitable, keep trying – do not give up!

After every loss, life still goes on. Life is a process and you are growing.

life is a progression of growth; and as believers we should be growing continuously into the nature and likeness of Christ.

Some of us are led to grow because we are hungry and thirsty for more of God, while for others, something tragic happen in their lives.

There are other times when growth is forced upon us because we go through a tough season, marital difficulty, a wayward child, the loss of a job, or some other losses in life.

One thing that is certain though is that God wants us to grow, and growth does not come easy; it can be extremely difficult. We do not just grow because we pray some prayer, no way. It's not that easy.

For you to gain spiritual insight or Godly wisdom and obtain all the things that God really wants you to acquire, you have got to go through some difficult situations. It might even be situations that you did not choose to go through, yet God will still guide you through.

It is time to grow. It is time to take on the challenges of life and trust God to see you through so that you can come out on the other side, and you can literally say "I have walked with God." I know it is scary, but you can trust God regardless of where you are, spiritually. God wants you to put His Word inside of you, in order to be strong, victorious, and a person of faith.

Darkness is universal, it is everywhere, and it can even be quite intimidating. Everything looks different in the dark, and when it really gets dark, you cannot see anything at all, just hang in there.

When we were younger, everyone wanted to grow up. We rarely hear about kids resisting growing up.

Growing up is a normal thing and believe me, growth is a good thing. Growing up really creeps up on you, and it happens without you even being aware.

Growth has a lot to do with your capability to endure different and difficult processes and to learn from life's experiences.

Most people don't realize how far they have grown and how developed they have become.

What are some of the signs that determine growth?

You have a better understanding of time

One of the obvious indications in life that you are growing is realizing the importance of time and how you manage it. This is a very important aspect of your life. Immature people don't really think about time and tend to waste a lot of it.

Ecclesiastes 3:1-2

There is a time for everything, and a season for every activity under the heavens; a time to be born and a time to die.

Everything in life has a beginning and an ending. There is always a close or an end to something and the beginning of something new. We all have one thing in common; from the day we were born, we were allotted a clock which ticks; those days will turn into weeks, the weeks months, the months years.

Think of how you spend your time.

Are you spending your time wisely, fulfilling your purpose, or are you wasting it being idle, pursing the things of this world? We were all given 24 hours a day, seven days a week; this is all we are going to get.

There are some that have done incredible things with their time, while there are others who do little with it. We can't blame the time spent or lack thereof on circumstances; we have trials and tribulations to overcome; we all have setbacks and delays.

We must wake up and start living our lives in purpose.

Time is too short and too valuable to waste.

If you continue wasting time and not pursuing purpose, you will end up with nothing but regrets, and regret is a terrible thing. You are setting yourself up to be sad and you will only regret things that you cannot ever go back in time to change. You cannot ever go back to do anything about what has already been done.

This is the perfect time to take control of your life; go through the growth process right now, take the opportunity to do the right thing and make the right choices; time is just too important to waste. If you do not like the path that your life is on, take steps of faith; you are the only one that can change it. You have what it takes because the greater One is living inside of you. God works through us.

One other way that we can stop wasting our time is to get rid of complaining. We waste so much time when we spend our days complaining. When we continue focusing and taking on our problems, they become magnified and appear even bigger than they really are. We will only become frustrated, angry, and bitter.

Instead of complaining, let us practice giving thanks. That is the only way to do it. Otherwise your whole life passes you by, and you will be living today, hoping for something that you do not have.

Let go of past hurts/learn to forgive

You know that you are growing when you refuse to waste time just living in the past. You cannot go back and redo anything in your life. So, let it go and move on and fulfill your destiny. You know God is not finished with you yet. It is never too late to start again.

Philip 3:12-14:

'Not that I have already obtained all this, or have already arrived at my goal, but I press on to take hold of that for which Christ Jesus took hold of me. Brothers and sisters, I do not consider myself yet to have taken hold of it. But one thing I do: Forgetting what is behind and straining toward what is ahead, I press on toward the goal to win the prize for which God has called me heavenward in Christ Jesus."

You need to get past the abuse, the pain, the rejection, the hurt from the past. You must stop talking about it; you must stop carrying it around. It is time you allowed that trauma from the past to be dead to you, you need to heal and go on. We are only given one life to live; let us leave a legacy for our children to carry. If you need a change in life, you are the one that must make it happen.

Your life is continually in the hands of the Creator of the universe, and you need to have the same determination to change.

There are people who are so quick to bring up, at the earliest opportunity, what friends and family did to hurt them in the past - things that happened five, ten, or fifteen years ago; we need to grow past those painful situations and let them go. God does not desire for us to be consumed with so much junk of our past.

You are growing when you learn to forgive, whether it is forgiving oneself or forgiving others.

As a mature believer, you must forgive the person who has done you wrong

Unforgiveness is like a bad seed planted in your garden of life. If it remains planted and never uprooted, it is going to grow roots and produce a negative outcome.

The product of unforgiveness will never disappear just because you start doing good things. Your good deeds are never enough to eliminate or to remove the bitterness, resentfulness, or unforgiveness you feel towards a person.

If you keep unforgiveness in your heart, it is a decision you are making not to walk in the fullness that God has for your life. If you remain resentful, it will only damage you. When you carry the weight of that unforgiveness and do not deal with it, you will never grow

If you have done something in your life and you just cannot forgive yourself, the consequences are still the same. It is still an attitude within you that carries condemnation, shame, guilt, and self-anger.

When you learn to forgive, it is one of the most liberating and self-loving things you will ever do. If you love yourself, you must forgive yourself

You Are Now Responsible

You are growing up and becoming a mature person when you learn how to confront responsibilities head-on. When you become responsible, God can trust you with anything. God will trust you with leadership, because He knows that you would not give up and throw in the towel when things get tough. He will trust you with wealth because He knows that you would not waste it, but rather be a good steward.

Everything in life begins with responsibility. The first responsibility in life is to be responsible to yourself. You must be responsible for your own life.

A person's character or level of maturity is measured by the ability to commit to responsibility. One of the first signs of a mature man or a woman is that such a person accepts responsibility. It is a responsible person that finishes what he has started.

It is time to take responsibility for your own life. You must take responsibility and crucify the flesh. It is your responsibility to fill up your spirit with the Word of God and grow in faith, knowledge, and prayer. You must take responsibility!!!

Choose the Right Friends

You are growing when your circle of friends is smaller. All relationships require energy and a part of growing up is realizing which relationships in your life truly hold value and which do not require your investing too much into them.

Mature people separate themselves from ungodly influences; they separate themselves from all bad influences that pull one down spiritually.

It is God's will for us to grow in that demonstration.

2 Peter 3:18 says: "Grow in the grace and knowledge of Jesus Christ."

Hebrews 6:1 says: "To leave the elementary doctrine of Christ and go on to maturity."

CHAPTER 8

THE WORD

We are in a spiritual battle for our hearts and mind, our families, our destiny, our careers, financial security and even our daily lives.

However, there is one who can empower you to prevail over the emotional, physical, and spiritual chaos in your life. There is one who can give you the power to be more than a conqueror; more than a winner; more than a victor,

We are all called to be overcomers, to walk in total victory and strength that comes from our heavenly father.

One might ask, how do we overcome?

The answer is we overcome everything through prayer and mediating on God's word.

So, no matter how messed up you feel, no matter what your messy situation is this day, you can overcome if you spend time in the presence of God.

Through prayer you will obtain victory, this is the glory of serving Jesus Christ.

There is a peace that passes all understanding that the Scripture talks about, and this is what God desires for all of us.

Yes, I know that the enemy wants to fill your heart with depression, anxiety, and fear. But I dare you to fear nothing because greater is He that is in you than he that is in the world.

I admonish you to find your identity in Christ Jesus.

You should never allow anyone to make you feel anything less than the champion that you are.

It does not matter whether they like you or not. It does not matter if they invite you to their dinner party or not.

It does not matter if their circle of friends approves of you or not – never change who you are to accommodate anyone.

The standard of life is the Word of God – live by the Word!!!

Allow the Word of God to infiltrate your life and change your direction and your destiny.

CONCLUSION

GROWING IN THE DARK

Overcoming the Dark

At one point or another, each of us have experienced a setback or went through a significant loss; perhaps that is where you are today; just maybe you have lost a job, a spouse, or even a love one or something you deeply care about.

If this is your situation, I want to encourage you. *In Matthew 5:4. Jesus says, "Blessed and enviably happy...are those who mourn, for they shall be comforted!"*

With this scripture I came to understand that our times of pain are perfect opportunities to receive and experience Gods supernatural comfort.

The comfort of God goes far beyond any ordinary kind of comfort. His love and grace are the only thing that can carry you through the darkest moments in your life, and help you to actually become a better, more powerful person than you were before.

With God's help, we can look at our dark days as opportunities to grow. We can have an attitude that says, "This may be difficult right now, but I will never quit, I will press in. I am really hurting, but I am going to survive this storm!"

There is definitely an appropriate time to grieve after a loss or tragedy, but we just do not want to get stuck there.

Just look at the life of Joseph. The Bible tells us his story in the book of Genesis.

As a young man, Joseph had great dreams for his life. But his older brothers hated him, they sold him into slavery. However, Joseph refused to give up.

He found great favor with his master, Potiphar, and was eventually put in charge of his entire household.

Joseph went from dark pit situation to the palace.

Yes, the Lord will often use others to comfort us. But even those people who are extremely close to us cannot give us everything we need all the time.

When we expect others to do for us what only God can do, we have our expectations in the wrong place, and we will always be disappointed.

However, the Bible says .... *"those who put their hope in the Lord will never be disappointed." (psalms 25:2).*

Psalm 34:18 says, "The Lord is close to those who are of a broken heart..."

He sees every hurt, every trial and every disappointment. And if we allow him, He will take the hurt and trauma that happened to us and work it out for our good.

I encourage you to never, ever give up on God. He is the only one who can take your pain and turn it into something great.

We often seek flawless or perfect conditions before we bud a new life.

We desire to see and understand how or even if we are growing.

It would be so great if all of our growth came with light, love, blue skies and green lights, where it feels amazing and we know exactly where we would end up.

I do not want to be the one to disappoint you, however, that is not the way it works.

The truth of the matter is, we were ordained to grow, one way or another.

The truth is that some of our most meaningful personal growth experiences can occur when life is the darkest, and times are mostly uncertain.

Nature and its wisdom have a lot to teach us about growth, let us look at the potato; the darkness does not seem to stifle the growth of a potato, or even a mushroom which grows buried deep under a pile of manure.

It is time for you to grow some new buds. Do not wait until your life is picture-perfect to grow, because it will never be that way.

Do not run away from your dark or hopeless times, learn from those seasons in life and invite the guidance of the Holy Spirit within you to reveal the meaning and purpose of the moment.

Allow every life experience to become your greatest teacher.

Continue pressing onward in your life and grow, regardless of the pain, evolve and grow into the remarkable human being that you are called to be.

www.ingramcontent.com/pod-product-compliance
Lightning Source LLC
Chambersburg PA
CBHW070057100426
42740CB00013B/2859